SEE YOU IN VALHALLA

OTHER BOOKS BY ROD MADOCKS

Fiction

No Way To Say Goodbye (2008)
Babbicam (2015)

Short Stories

Ship of Fools: Stories From The Mental Health Front Line (2013)

Memoir

The Rising Flame: Remembering Sidney Keyes (2015)
Our Tan: Memoir of a Destroyed Life (2018)
Muzungu: A Rhodesian Testament (2022)

SEE YOU IN VALHALLA

A Centenary Tribute to Sidney Keyes

ROD MADOCKS

Shoestring  Press

Printed by imprintdigital
Upton Pyne, Exeter
www.digital.imprint.co.uk

Typesetting and cover design by The Book Typesetters
us@thebooktypesetters.com
07422 598 168
www.thebooktypesetters.com

Published by Shoestring Press
19 Devonshire Avenue, Beeston, Nottingham, NG9 1BS
0115 925 1827
www.shoestringpress.co.uk

First published 2022
© Copyright: Rod Madocks
© Cover illustration: Estate of John Craxton. All rights reserved
DACS 2022.

ISBN 978-1-915553-02-7

In Memory of S.A.K.K.
and his fallen comrades in
The Queens Own Royal West Kents.

Sidney Keyes & Milein Cosman, Oxford, 1941

"See you in the spring or in Walhall."
Pencilled note left by Sidney Keyes for
Milein Cosman, January 1943, on the eve
of his going to war.

CONTENTS

See You in Valhalla

I

Sidney Keyes, was born on 27th May 1922. We have had a hundred years of his voice if not the man. His was the generation called to war, their necks haltered and their tongues "schooled in words of fear".[1] Keyes wrote in his second collection of poems, published after his death,

> Tonight the stranger city and the old
> Moon that stands over it proclaim
> A cruel solstice, coming ice and cold
> Thoughts and the darkening of the heart's flame.[2]

In that same year, Keyes told his friend, the poet, John Heath-Stubbs, that he saw his own life as "a restless candle flame rising clearest at its moment of extinction"[3]. His work is full of images of stranded instants between heaves of storm, unmoored moments of stillness and brief licks of light. Reading Keyes, I often think of that image from Langland's 'Piers Plowman' about the life of man as "… a kex or candle that caught hath fire and blazeth"[4].

I see Keyes not so much a war poet but a youthful prodigy, brimming with genius and spurred on by a louring fate, "a barb of light" as he also described fellow doomed souls in his long poem, 'The Foreign Gate' (1942). He faced necrophilous times and a sacrificial inferno into which were also cast his contemporaries and confrères, Keith Douglas, Alun Lewis and Drummond Allison. Valhalla, the Norse abode for fallen heroes, is mentioned quite a few times in Keyes' work. It's clear he viewed this supposed resting place for warriors in a bitter and ironic way. To him, it was a place of immemorial chill and desolate exile where "lonely and inhuman kings … sit with drawn-up knees/ waiting

---

[1] Sidney Keyes, 'Not Chosen', (1942)

[2] Sidney Keyes, 'The Cruel Solstice', (1942)

[3] Sidney Keyes, Letter printed in *Minos of Crete* (1948)

[4] William Langland, *Piers Plowman* (c. 1377)

with twisted eyes the time of terror".[5]

It's been a hundred years since his birth in a late spring in Kent. Keyes himself was well aware of the power of anniversaries. He was conscious from a young age that he was running short of time and the marking of the returning cycle of the seasons and noting of anniversaries were particularly important to him. His poem, 'A Garland for John Clare', written when he was nineteen, takes the form of an imagined conversation with the Northamptonshire poet and a plea to borrow from his courage. Keyes dated the poem "12th–13th July, 1941". This was Clare's birthday. I'm sure that Keyes also knew that day in 1941 was the 100th anniversary of Clare's famous eighty mile walk from his Epping asylum back to his home village. Keyes' poem refers to both poets enduring "time's contempt for such as you and I" and praising Clare for "driving the coulter … not marking how the soil closed its cut grin behind you." Clare was forsaken by friends and condemned to the years of forgetting due to madness and confinement and Keyes was defrauded of his due time and fame by war but still driving his coulter hard and deep right up to the end.

Keyes is now seen as a fugatory, minor figure in the history of English poetry, a student rhymer whose life was snatched away too early by war. He is often consigned to the lost property office of prematurely-curtailed poetic talent. I'm arguing for him to be recognised as something much more substantial. He rode his fleeting moments of literary fame to the utmost and left a voice that lingers in the memory. The life was also admirable, a force-field among his contemporaries, the artist nerving himself to go beyond fear and face the inevitable.

Take this then in turn as my centenary garland for Sidney Arthur Kilworth Keyes, known as 'Mick' to his family.

---

[5] Sidney Keyes, 'Troll Kings', (1941)

II

Sidney Keyes was born in Dartford, Kent. His mother died shortly after he was born. He told friends that he had a vestigial infant's memory, real or imagined, of being taken to hospital to see her as she lay dying in hospital. His father had been an infantry captain in the Great War. One has the impression he was a damaged man, seemingly unable to cope with bringing up a son. He was thrice married and with T.B. eating into him throughout Keyes' early years. The lad was largely brought up at his grandfather's farmhouse near Dartford. He was home-schooled for years, a lonely child in a large house. Keyes knew the names of all the plants and creatures he encountered. He kept foundling orphaned hedgehogs and field mice in his bedroom for company as he pored over his favourite reading: history books and accounts of myths and legends.

His childhood was dominated by his grandfather, a self-made yeoman farmer, also three times married, who ran a successful milling business. Something about the loss of his mother, the succession of nannies and step-mothers combining with the dominating psychic heft of his grandfather gave Keyes an abiding sense of guilt and fear that you can see evidenced early on in his writing. A remarkable poem written at the age of sixteen about his grandfather's death contains so many Keyesian themes: the compressed urgency, the sense of unspoken threats, the elegiac tone that becomes an anti-elegy when combined with a steeliness of vision.

> April again and it is a year again …..
> Since they gave you to the worms.
> I am ashamed to take delight in these rhymes
> Without grief; but you need no tears,
> We shall never escape or forget you, nor make terms
> With your enemies, the swift departing years.[6]

---

[6] Sidney Keyes, 'Elegy', (1938)

A new step-mother, Violet Keyes, insisted that Keyes attend mainstream schooling, and he was sent to Dartford Grammar School in his teenage years. The school helped bring him out of isolation. He learned French and German and excelled at drama and the spoken word, and the school was still close to the nearby fields and woods that he loved. In 1935, he went on to Tonbridge School where his poetic talents were further recognized by a sympathetic school master, the poet Tom Staveley, who also helped Keyes make a formative lone trip to France. He returned from there on one of the last boat trains on the eve of war when he was not quite eighteen.

He won a scholarship to Queens' College, Oxford to study history and went up in October 1940. There, he met John Heath Stubbs, Drummond Allison and Michael Meyer, the group forming a literary coterie, cross-influencing each other and sharing a love for the Romantic Poets, for Yeats and Rilke. Keyes particularly loved the fierce, pagan archetypes and the heroes that triumph over darkness to be found in the works of Karl Jung. John Heath-Stubbs seems to be the strongest influence of the group, persuading Keyes to concentrate on poetry and to admire the obscure sacral writings of the now almost forgotten Charles Williams. T.S. Eliot seems to have been a particular influence on Keyes.[7] There are many Eliot echoes in tone and imagery in Keyes' work. I note for example that Keyes' poem 'Advice for a Journey' (1941) which has the lines, "never look back nor too far forward... go on , go out...," is dated one month after Eliot's 'Dry Salvages' sequence came out in Faber pamphlet form in February 1941 with a similar call to those facing an uncertain, calamitous future: "O voyagers, o seamen..... Not fare well, but fare forward."

Most importantly, Keyes met the artist, Milein Cosman in his first year at Oxford. She was his own age, studying at The Slade but temporarily located in Oxford due to The Blitz. She was from a refugee German family and became Keyes' unwilling muse. He fell deeply in love with her but these feelings was not returned. Keyes never really lost his love for her. She kept the friendship

---

[7] Keyes acknowledged Eliot as one among a number of "Explorers" in the dedication to 'The Wilderness' (1942/3).

and we are indebted to her memory for letting him pour out so many illuminating letters and poems to her. She allowed Keyes to enter a long tradition that stretches from Sappho to Keats and beyond, poems about the trajectory of thwarted love. Eros is most often associated with lack, loss and absence as Anne Carson observes[8] and Keyes, a doomy, macabre-obsessed *pierrot* figure during his student days, perfectly lived up to that tradition. He seemed always to be interrogating the vacuum left by the love object much as his contemporary, Alun Lewis, also expressed it: "the single poetic theme of Life and Death … the question of what survives of the beloved".[9] Keyes and Lewis in fact corresponded together and arranged to meet but this never came about as Lewis was suddenly posted with his unit to India.

That hard winter of 1940/41, the war increasingly impinged on Keyes and all his generation, those that had chosen to stay and see it through, that is. There was the case of W.H. Auden, safe in New York, writing hortatory poems like 'September 1st 1939': I sit in one of the dives/ On Fifty-second Street/Uncertain and afraid/As the clever hopes expire/Of a low dishonest decade." You can imagine what Keyes and his friends thought of those lines as they received their call-up papers that winter.

Keyes worked hard, supercharging each moment. Many observers saw him in the midst of undergraduate parties and music concerts, always sitting in corners busily writing his verses. As well as attending his studies and bombarding Milein with love poems, he also put on a performance of a play he had written, and was a co-editor of *Cherwell* newspaper, and in 1941 he and Michael Meyer put together the poetry collection that became *Eight Oxford Poets* published by Routledge under the mentorship of Herbert Read in 1941 – a slim, handsome soft-back with a brick-red cover and gold lettering containing poems from Keyes, Michael Meyer, J.A. Shaw, Drummond Allison, Roy Porter, John Heath-Stubbs, Gordon Swaine and Keith Douglas. All contributors were Oxford undergraduates at the time. Keyes wrote in the Foreword that the

---

[8] Anne Carson, *Eros the Bittersweet: An Essay*, Princeton U.P.(1986)

[9] Alun Lewis, Letter, (1943), *In The Green Tree: The Letters & Short Stories of Alun Lewis*, Parthian Bks, (2006)

selected poets: "share a horror at the world's predicament together with the feeling that we cannot save ourselves without some kind of spiritual readjustment." They shared some features: they were searching for a new lyric focus and rejected the evidently political gaze of Auden. Keyes further wrote in the Foreword that they were: "romantic writers and we have, on the whole, little sympathy with the Audenian school of poets." They have come to be seen as part of the 'Neo-Romantic' movement although many of them later rejected that label in one way or another.

James Keery identifies a distinction to be drawn between the familiar 'ironic modernism' epitomised by Auden and an alternative vein of 'visionary modernism'[10] The 'visionary modernism' of the Apocalypse movement fits the Oxford Eight better than 'Neo-Romantics' for all the 'floridity' that Keyes himself acknowledged in his Foreword to the anthology. Their poems share a sense of high-flown dread, an immersion in the metaphysical potentiality of nature, a sense of a molten world that flares with surreal intensities. So many of the poets of their generation were similarly groping for a fresh poetic vocabulary. One young poet, Brian Allwood, wrote in a 1943 literary review "I think most people still feel Auden looking over their shoulder and they don't know which way to run. In which direction will the new hegira be?"[11]

Allwood was to be killed with the R.A.F. in Italy in 1944 and of the writers collected in the Oxford anthology three were to die in the war and three would later abandon poetry. Famously, Philip Larkin, also at Oxford at the time and protected from war service by poor eyesight, was not included in the anthology and felt resentment about it. He later wrote about perceived pretentiousness and unnecessary classical allusions in Keyes' and John Heath Stubbs' work, although his own early work also showed neo- romantic/apocalyptic traits. Larkin later abjured the visionary apocalyptic mindset, preferring instead to dwell on private moments– "we are not suited to the long perspectives."[12]

---

[10] James Keery, *Introduction to Apocalypse: an Anthology*, Carcanet (2020)

[11] Brian Alwood quoted in *The Poetry of the Forties* by A. T. Tolley (1985)

Much later, he described how he met Keyes in an Oxford street in 1941. Keyes was wearing an unusual Russian fur hat (he always felt the cold keenly). Larkin could recall little of the conversation between them. What he most remembered was the disturbing impression of Keyes' "most remarkable large brown piercing eyes"[13]

Reading *Eight Oxford Poets* now, it is Keyes' bitter vatic voice that stands out most strongly among his fellow contributors, even though Keith Douglas, for example, would be given more time to grow into being a much stronger poet. That intensity seems to have come from Keyes' self-belief and drive to develop his talent while he could. *Eight Oxford Poets* received good reviews and Keyes' contribution was particularly admired, Edwin Muir wrote in *The Listener*: "Obviously a poet of original talent ... all his poetry has shape, significance and fine precision of imagery." Keyes was beginning to be recognised and that late winter he contributed poems to *The New Statesman*, *Horizon* and *The Listener*. In the early months of 1942 he assembled his first collection, *The Iron Laurel* also to be published by Routledge. He began to be seen as a spokesperson for a young generation of writers and was asked to contribute to a book of essays to be published as *The Future of Faith* edited by Percy Colson. Keyes entitled his essay 'The Artist in Society' and stated there that the purpose of the artist was to: "reveal to the rest of humanity important aspects of reality which otherwise they could never have known". He further commented that the point of art lay not in self-expression or doctrinal preaching but rather in the Rilkean notion of "letting the world express him and ... giving himself entirely to something outside himself."[14]

Keyes was called up in the middle of term in his second year at Queens, and in April 1942 he commenced his initial training at Infantry No. 25 Training Centre, Omagh, County Tyrone. Here a personal note enters: my father, J.E. Madocks, also nineteen

---

[12] Philip Larkin, 'Reference Back' *Whitsun Weddings*, Faber (1955)

[13] Philip Larkin, *The North Ship* Foreword to 1966 Faber edition

[14] Sidney Keyes, 'The Artist in Society' reprinted in *Minos of Crete* (1948)

years old and called up in his second year at university, was on that troop train which carried Keyes to Omagh. He watched the military police confiscating Keyes' poetry manuscripts and German books and found himself in an adjoining bunk in the intake Nissen hut which his draft all shared. Dad told me all about Sidney Keyes from when I was young. He never forgot how he was briefly a comrade and friend to the famed poet. He told me also about Keyes' unhandiness as a soldier, how he was constantly harried by the drill sergeants for sloppiness and how the actor, Trevor Howard, also training with them, liked to bully and make fun of the absent-minded poet. All the while, at every pause in their duties when the rest chatted, smoked and played cards, Keyes was to be seen reading or scribbling in his notebooks. Dad told me how the experienced men and those more fitted to the military life shook their heads over the poet. They hoped Keyes would find a safe desk job in something like the Intelligence Corps as he seemed doomed to swiftly getting the chop in the meat-grinder infantry war. Yet despite his clumsiness there was something steely in the poet's gaze and in his readiness to go the distance.

A few notebook entries and letters to friends do show that, in a strange way, the army appealed to Keyes' sense of dedication, his emotional asceticism, and his tough, somewhat inflexible personality. He wrote to John Heath Stubbs, "a vision of the army as it strikes me – cold, obscenity, tiredness, an occasional sense of peace greater than I have known before."[15] Perhaps the army helped him lose some of his undergraduate, high-romanticism. He kept on producing poems at an impressive rate; the work was deepening and a fatalistic tone emerged: "all must face the sun, the red rock desert / and see the burning of the metal bird", prescient lines from his long poem, 'The Wilderness' (1942/43). He kept up his hopeless yearning for Milein and tried making trunk calls to her through cumbersome wartime phone exchanges, calls that were rarely answered. He wrote his memorable poem dedicated to her called 'Not Chosen' with its last lines: "O take me back, but as you take remember/ My love will bring you

---

[15] Sidney Keyes, 1942 Letter, quoted by John Guenther, *Sidney Keyes: A Biographical Enquiry*, London Magazine Editions, (1967)

nothing but trouble my dear." He told John Heath-Stubbs that he had found a copy of Catullus' caustic misogynistic verses in a local library and translated the following lines from 'Carmen XI': "my love's like any flower of the fallow/ cut down and wasted by the passing plow."[16]

Keyes' intake shipped out for a second phase of more extensive officer cadet training known as O.C.T.U. Indeed, in a letter at the time Keyes coined the apt descriptive phrase about his undergraduate peer group, "We are the O.C.T.U. generation" (I have never found the exact source of the quote although it is often cited). This training took place at Dunbar on the south east coast of Scotland. My father left me a note cached inside his copy of *The Collected Poems* edited by Michael Meyer, 1945. In it, he describing sharing a room with Keyes at the Royal Hotel, Dunbar (taken over by the army during wartime). He recounted how in their free hours Keyes was always writing and sometimes he discussed his latest poems with Dad, who wrote that the poem 'Dunbar, 1650' had been inspired by Keyes' historical sense sparked after they had completed a military exercise on the site of the Cromwellian battle on nearby Doon Hill. Dad also told how Keyes gave him a signed copy of *The Iron Laurel*. He later took it with him when he embarked on D-Day, the invasion of Normandy in June 1944, but it was subsequently stolen from his kit. Also on that piece of paper, Dad copied out these lines that had been written in their shared room at Dunbar and which had special significance to him:

> O never weep for me, my love,
> Or seek me in this land:
> But light a candle for my luck
> And bear it in your hand.[17]

---

[16] Sidney Keyes, later revised and published in *The Cruel Solstice* collection with the date of 'May, 1942'.

[17] Sidney Keyes, 'The Wilderness', (1942)

III

O.C.T.U. training ended that autumn of 1942. Keyes bid farewell to my father. They shook hands and were never to meet again. Keyes joined the Queen's Own Royal West Kent regiment, his father's old unit, which was then training to take part in the final phase of the North African campaign. Keyes became a junior subaltern in an infantry platoon. His men seemed to like him, they nicknamed him 'Puss in Boots' in reference to his rubber-soled footwear and to something in his manner. The pace of training accelerated and there were fewer opportunities for leave. Keyes was still bound up in his relentless adoration of Milein. She had declined to spend time with him in London during July 1942 and he had commenced an affair with her roommate in Oxford, another painter, Renée-Jane Scott. A warm and generous woman, she kept company with Keyes when he revisited his childhood haunts: "the feeling of autumn is so strong that I must go where I have felt it the most strongly in the past, the great damp woods of the Weald"[18]

We should be thankful to the memory of Renée-Jane; there are at least two Keyes poems dedicated to her, including 'Seascape'(1942) , inspired by one of her paintings, which has the ominous first line "Our country was a country drowned long since". I am indebted to the writer, Adrian Caesar, for generously sharing his insights on Renée-Jane with me. He told me he met her in 1980 while he was researching Keyes for his Ph.D. thesis, some parts of which later became Caesar's book, *Dividing Lines: Poetry, Class and Ideology in the 1930s* (1991).

Adrian confirmed to me that Renée-Jane's relationship with Keyes did not run smoothly, there was a rival for her affections yet she apparently agreed to write to Keyes while he was at war until such a time he might be killed.

In a similar realistic mood in the first months of 1943, Keyes assembled his final collection, *The Cruel Solstice*, and dedicated it to John Heath-Stubbs. He visited Oxford for the last time and

---

[18] Sidney Keyes, Notebook, *Minos of Crete*

climbed the creaking stair to No. 3 St. John Street, Milein Cosman's rooms, leaving that note on her mantel: "see you in the spring or in Walhall". He also saw Herbert Read in London to deposit manuscripts. Read wrote later in the Foreword to the 1947 American edition of *The Collected Poems of Sidney Keyes*: "When he came to say goodbye he did it with an air of finality which at the time I thought he had assumed as a shield against false hope."

Keyes took ship on the 16th March bound for Algiers. He must have been reading Rilke's prose novel *The Notebook of Malte Laurids Brigge* because he borrowed an idea from that work when he wrote in his notebook about how everyone carries their death inside them waiting for it to hatch out in its due time. He also wrote that he had achieved a peacefulness on board, photos of Milein and Renée-Jane pinned above his bunk: "the succession of days, like a dream, is infinitely soothing", noting that he had come to realise that, every moment is a state of being in itself not a way of transition into a next"[19].

He arrived with a bang in the middle of a German air raid on the port. His men were impressed by his coolness under this first bout of fire. One of the privates in his platoon, James Lucas, (later to work at the Imperial War Museum) left a brief memoir of Keyes at war that appeared in the 1988 Carcanet edition of *The Collected Poems*[20] Keyes and his men joined the 1st Battalion of the West Kents in the Tunisian mountains where the British 1st Army had been stalled up all winter in the hills around Medjez-el-Bab, thirty miles from Tunis. Although in retreat after a renewed British offensive, the Germans still made fierce counter-attacks and the casualty rate was high. This was not the desert nor "the red rock wilderness" as imagined in Keyes' last published poem. The landscape was bright green with wild wheat and wreathed in spring plants and flowers. Keyes wrote to Renée-Jane that he had, "a most strange and unlucky dream ... I dreamt that we were married and I saw the actual ceremony. This is said to be one of the most

---

19 *Ibid.*

20 James Lucas also wrote a longer piece about his service with Keyes that was published as 'Point 133 Tunisia' in *War Monthly* magazine (1980, No. 56).

unlucky dreams to have."[21]

He went up to the line shortly after writing that and within two weeks he was dead. We know he wrote poems but nothing survives of them. On 28th April, his unit made a night attack on Hill 133, an attempt to crack open the last German positions on high ground blocking the way to Massicault and Tunis beyond. The precise details about how he came to be killed have never been established. I have written in more detail about what might have happened in *The Rising Flame*. He seems to have vanished in the storm of the roaring world like the Rilkean hero in his favourite Elegy 6 of *The Duino Elegies*. After a further two weeks, the Germans had given way and the campaign in North Africa was over. It was months before a gravesite was identified, a mile beyond the point where Keyes was last seen. The Army Graves Registration Unit gave a date of 29th April for his death. It seemed fitting: "April again….and we have fallen on bad times".[22] In the course of writing this piece, I've found a record in the Register of Marriages for April 1943 that Renée-Jane Scott married Mr. Johnson. Yes, Keyes' lover was married to someone else before it was even definitively known that he had been killed. It makes me think of the last lines in one of his last known completed poems:

> We do not know the end, we cannot tell
> That valley's shape nor whether the white fire
> Will blind us instantly ….
> > Only we go
> Forward, we go forward together, leaving
> Nothing except a worn-out way of loving.[23]

---

[21] Sidney Keyes, Letter, quoted by Guenther, *op. cit.*

[22] From Keyes' first published poem, 'Elegy', in memory of his grandfather who also carried the initials S.K.K.

[23] Sidney Keyes, 'The Wilderness', (December 1942/ January 1943)

IV

Keyes was visibly changed by army life. He became tougher or it could be said that the army simply stripped back the extraneous and revealed his stony inner resilience; "I grow colder and drier", he noted to Renée-Jane in one of the last letters from England.[24]; his eyes had become "barbed" as he foretold in 'War Poet' (March 1942) and his hands now, "heavy… (with)… new precision" from handling weapons ('Not Chosen', July 1942). He certainly became more taciturn and there were fewer poems some of them like 'An Early Death' written in early '43 are maybe among his best. We have no evidence of him displaying the mordant jokiness that was such a feature in World War Two military speech and which is reflected in, say, Douglas' poems, although Keyes could play dark jokes. Lucas tells us in his Carcanet memoir that when posted to the front on the battleground called 'Banana Ridge', Keyes had become tired of two mouthy sergeants who kept going on about wanting to kill Germans. Apparently, he took the two sergeants out with him on night patrol into the spooky terrain of no-man's-land and left them to stew in the dark while he crawled away alone further towards the Germans. Keyes returned at dawn to rescue the chastened, silenced men.

He remained an awkward, unmilitary-looking figure though he traded on his courage and spoke humanly and candidly to his men. He eschewed military bluster, sometimes apologising if he got things wrong. His last recorded conversation was to warn James Lucas about German anti-personnel 'S' mines. Keyes gave him hard-bitten advice to keep his foot on the mine if he triggered one, telling him the secondary charge would likely blow off his foot but it would save everyone else from being hit by shrapnel.[25] This is not the Keyes characterised by Clive James as, "a type of swot…immature even beyond his years …a large-lipped fish out of water. It's easy to imagine him …on patrol…Keyes mooning along"[26]. There have been so many other attacks on Keyes, I've

[24] Sidney Keyes, Letter, reprinted by Guenther, *op. cit.*
[25] James Lucas, 'Point 133 Tunisia', *op. cit.*

collected some of the phrases from many sources: *a tin ear, hammy, lacking plain roots.* Well sure, so many of his poems are him trying out his wings, but for a man facing the unendurable and still cranking out commendable poems he was also admirable. Anyway, who else is to speak up for Keyes a hundred years after?

Keyes was actually born on the very same day as the actor Christopher Lee and Lee's long career has always reminded me of all the potential life and achievement that Keyes missed out on. Lee became an intelligence officer in the R.A.F. during the war and there is evidence that he latterly embellished his accounts of his war career, claiming to have been in the S.A.S. and Special Forces, rather as the actor Trevor Howard, who enjoyed tormenting Keyes at O.C.T.U. also claimed to have had a heroic military career despite being thrown out of the army in 1943 as being 'psychologically unsuitable'. Had he survived, Keyes at least would not have needed to lie about his combat experience, and overall there is an intense straightness and honesty about him and his work.

I'm thinking of that image in Keith Douglas' poem 'How To Kill' ('1943') "under the parabola of a ball/ a child turning into a man". In the poem, a thrown ball lofts upward and casts a shadow over a running child who stares up too long at the sky as he fumbles to catch the projectile. That ball in time becoming a grenade then the optical gunsight of the tank gunner who delivers the shadow of death on his enemy yet who also knows that the mosquito death will as easily shadow him. The imagery comes from Rilke's *Sonnets to Orpheus* Book Two, Elegy 8 as well as his poem 'Das Kind'.

Both Douglas and Keyes were under Rilke's spell. How often I've thought of both poets trying to outrun that falling shadow, all the while accompanied by the doomy tread of Rilke's incantations: *ein Mal/ jedes, nur ein Mal, ein Mal und nichtmehr…*("once for each of us, only once, and nothing more"[27]

---

[26] Essay reprinted in *The Metropolitan Critic* (1974, rpr. 2015)

[27] R.M. Rilke 9th Elegy, *The Duino Elegies* (1923)

My father inducted me into appreciating Keyes or maybe he simply made it easy for Keyes to choose me. I'm of Keyes' party. How could I not be? For all that, I try and see him clear. I thought I'd said everything I'd wanted to about the poet in *The Rising Flame: Remembering Sidney Keyes*[28] yet he still calls to me and I've come to understand new things about his work. His plangent, bitter voice seems more relevant than ever now especially to one growing older and whose dreams are shredding out to nothing. Keyes certainly seemed clear-eyed about 'love' for all his youth, he seems to have divined the innate ferocity of sex and to have reconciled himself to the wintry pleasures of disappointed love. Keyes' personal story of courage also inspires me, his squaring to face things and his struggle to get control over time. His poems are literal and candid for all their ornamentation. Reading them again, they help me stay ahead of my own losses and as I read I seem to feel his calm yet implacable eyes looking me through and through. For Keyes, it was "the necrophilous Germans…(and)… the European Death Wish"[29] and for us it is the fleeting years, pandemics, war and climate change. Keyes is my expert in how to face and transcend a malignant future.

---

[28] Rod Madocks, Shoestring Press (2015)

[29] Sidney Keyes, Letter, March 1943 to John Heath Stubbs, reprinted in Guenther, *op. cit.*

V

Sidney Keyes was popular among his contemporaries especially the O.C.T.U. generation of young officers. Edmund Blunden reported that in 1944 he had heard public schoolboys quoting from 'Remember Your Lovers' from memory.[30] There was an implicit class dimension to Keyes' contemporary appeal, he was after all a member of the officer class although he showed no interest in social categories or politics of any hue and thought of himself as an 'outsider' figure. Men in his world lived to be sacrificed. They had a rendezvous with "sleep's cruel brother" – death ('Four Postures of Death', 1942), and women in his work, when not somehow seeking the blood of their young men, were assigned the role of muses or observers of the arid fate of their menfolk. The distinctive Second World War element I think of much of Keyes' appeal to his contemporaries lay in the austerity of his vision. His verse might be ornamented but his poetic landscape was shorn of any mention of God or country or even of the succour of comradeship that was so strong a feature of the previous war's poetry. He exhorted his O.C.T.U. companions to go out alone into: "the bad lands of battle, into the cloud-wall/ of the future, my friends, and leave your fear."[31]

The Cruel Solstice earned Keyes a posthumous Hawthornden prize in 1944 and for a while he was hailed as the new Rupert Brookes. He was perhaps over-hyped at the time and so his name fell away the more quickly once the war ended. Those who had read him more carefully saw him as not being so much a war poet but as Edmund Blunden observed, a writer feeding off a "larger commotion and dissonance of which war is a partial embodiment".[32] In time, Keith Douglas, Alun Lewis, Alan Ross, Sorley MacLean and others became more favoured as representatives of the best in World War Two poetry. High-flown Keyesian intensity along with oracular Yeats and the metaphysics

---

[30] Cited in A. T. Tolley, *Poetry of the 1940s*, *op. cit.*

[31] Sidney Keyes, 'Advice for a Journey', 1941

[32] Edmund Blunden quoted in Guenther, *op. cit.*

and cloudy symbolism of Rilke went out of fashion in the demotic post-war world. Keyes' name ebbed as the war generation died out, my father among them. His reputation resurged a little with the 1988 Carcanet edition of *Sidney Keyes: Collected Poems* and more recently his legacy has been reconsidered. In 2013, John Lucas identified the "bardic" quality of Keyes' "rapt hieratic voice" that contrasted with Douglas' often "sardonic, aghast brutally comic" tone. Lucas pointed out: "it isn't difficult to imagine the young Geoffrey Hill reading … (Keyes' 'The Foreign Gate') … and seeing … a way to go forward with his own engagements with English history."[33]

Hill was to write an appreciation of Keyes in 'Sidney Keyes in Historical Perspective'[34] where he argued that the undercutting and contesting of themes in Keyes' interplay between pastoral manqué and metaphysical elements in his work were "signs of potential greatness in a poet". Hill's own *Tenebrae* 1978 collection seem to me to contain his most Keyesian poems, full of candle flame images and dramatic contrapuntal voices and the shadow of Keyes is ever-present in Hill's last published sequence published posthumously in 2019 – *The Book of Baruch by the Gnostic Justin*. I can't think of any that carry on that tradition. Tom Paulin's notorious attack on Hill being part of a "shabby and reactionary hegemony" and citing his less-than-perfect ear… (his)… *aestheticism* …(and Hill being) … a parasite on Eliot"[35] mirrors similar post-war criticism on Keyes' work.

You can still find Keyes admirers here and there. Michael Tippet combined 'Remember Your Lovers' with a piece by Alun Lewis in his 'The Heart's Assurance' 1950 song cycle. Ronald Blythe cited Keyes' 'A Garland for John Clare' as his favourite poem about Clare[36]. Readers of Richard Adams' 'Watership Down' (1972) would have noticed a quote from

[33] John Lucas, *Second World War Poetry in English*, Greenwich Exchange (2013)

[34] Tim Kendall, ed. *The Oxford Handbook of British and Irish War Poetry* (2007)

[35] Tom Paulin, 'The Case for Geoffrey Hill' in *The London Review of Books*, (April, 1985)

[36] Ronald Blythe, *Talking About John Clare*, Trent Books, (1999)

'Death and the Maiden' as a chapter epigraph. More recently, the Irish poet, Kevin Higgins, in his poem 'Got: After Sidney Keyes'[37] riffs Keyes' 'War Poet' to make a rueful poem about living through Covid times. Four Keyes poems feature in James Keery's new collection of apocalypse poetry[38] and it was instructive to see them as part of a sweep of 'visionary modernist' writing. Keery drily points out the persistence of negative attitudes toward the school of neo-romantic/apocalyptic writing; he cites as an example Michael Hofman's introduction to *W.S. Graham: Selected Poems* (2018) where Hofman deplores "the awful British new romantics"[39]. Well, for good or ill, awful or not, we are still on the post-Auden hegira, my friends, "never look back nor too far forward".

I read from this Keyes' poem at my father's funeral:

"This is the day his death will be remembered
…..the healing hands lie folded like dead birds:
Their stillness is our comfort who have seen him."[40]

I'd first begun to immerse myself in Keyes as an honouring of both of them, and I've tried to set a seal on that living link which first connected them at Infantry Training Camp No.25 in Omagh. I thought I'd discharged that task but Keyes still visits me as he did his friend John Heath-Stubbs like: "a bird returning to a darkened window / the hard-eyed albatross with a scissored bill"[41]

Keyes stays with me. Heath-Stubbs spoke of his implicit fear of Keyes. It's something I also feel. Fear yes, Keyes' cold heroes and dark themes trouble me and he was so much more intensely fierce than many realised and more fit than they supposed to gain admittance to *Walhall*.

---

[37] Kevin Higgins in the on-line journal, *http://pendemic.ie/* (2020)

[38] *Apocalypse: An Anthology, op. cit.*

[39] *Ibid.*

[40] Sidney Keyes, Advice for a Journey, (1941)

[41] John Heath-Stubbs, 'In Memory of Sidney Keyes', *The Divided Ways* (1946)

Et in Arcadia ego might well have suited Keyes as a motto.[42] Literally meaning: "And I also exist in Arcadia". I'm often reminded of the tag when revisiting Keyes' mordant, lyrical lines. The phrase and Keyes' poems still speak to our current times: I (Death) lurk in all your Shangri-Las and supposed 'safe spaces'.

Maybe I'll try and lay his stony ghost someday by going to the Tunisian mountains when they are green with spring wheat, the *garrigue* flowering on the high places. I'll explore Banana Ridge where Keyes crawled about in no-man's-land inspecting unusual beetles on a dead dog and where he scared the mouthy sergeants, and go on to the fatal Hill 133 where he led his men into the inscrutable darkness. I'd also like to visit the grave in Massicault military cemetery and leave some Kentish wildflowers there. But is it really him under that headstone? He's really in no place, somewhere at sea, like those drowned figures in so many of his poems. 'Glaucus' for instance, written in November 1941.

Glaucus, one of those classical references that Larkin complained about in Keyes' work, a merman and an immortal with the gift of prophesy raised by Aesculapius from the dead. Keyes probably knew of him from Ovid's *Metamorphoses*. Glaucus loved the divine Scylla and not being loved in return, was doomed to drift in the oceans offering warnings and prognostications to passing sailors. In the poem, Keyes describes Glaucus as "gull-swift and swerving, the wet spirit freed."[43] Thus it is in the form of Glaucus that I most often think of Keyes when revisiting the coast at Dartford and Dunbar and most of all at Zennor where his friend, the blind poet, John Heath-Stubbs, once lived. I've often walked westward out from the cramped hamlet of Zennor to those dark basaltic cliffs that overlook a harsh sea. Sometimes I seem to glimpse there an unresting petrel spirit flitting on over the waters.

[42] Irwin Panofsky best explicated the phrase and linked it to the implicit tragedy of the pastoral. I wonder if Keyes read his essay in *Philosophy and History*, ed R. Kibansky, Oxford, 1936.

[43] Sidney Keyes, 'Glaucus' (1941)

Sidney Keyes:
Selected Poems Referenced
in the Text

ELEGY

(In memoriam S.K.K)

April again, and it is a year again
Since you walked out and slammed the door
Leaving us tangled in your words. Your brain
Lives in the bank-book, and your eyes look up
Laughing from the carpet on the floor:
And we still drink from your silver cup.

It is a year again since they poured
The dumb ground into your mouth:
And yet we know, by some recurring word
Or look caught unawares, that you still drive
Our thoughts like the smart cobs of your youth –
When you and the world were alive.

A year again, and we have fallen on bad times
Since they gave you to the worms.
I am ashamed to take delight in these rhymes
Without grief; but you need no tears.
We who never forget nor escape you, nor make terms
With your enemies, the swift departing years.

July 1938

THE CRUEL SOLSTICE

Tonight the stranger city and the old
Moon that stands over it proclaim
A cruel solstice, coming ice and cold
Thoughts and the darkening of the heart's flame

'Stand up,' speaks soul, 'let wisdom turn the time'
Into an image of your day's 'despite';
O clever soul, we were born separate,
Held only in hard glance or studied rhyme.

'Sleep then, tired singer, stop the mouth
Of the unhappy month and take your rest.'
O cunning voice, I have not strength enough
Being no stranger here, but uncouth guest.

So must I walk or falter by the wall
Wondering at my own impotence
Of thought and action; at the fall
Of love and cities and the heart's false diligence.

Tonight I cannot speak, remembering
For all my daily talk, I dare not enter
The empty month; can only stand and think
Of you, my dearest, and the approaching winter.

GLAUCUS

The various voices are his poem now.
Under the currents, under the shifting lights
Of midway water, rolls his fleshy wreck:
Its gurnard eye reflects those airy heights
Where once it noted white Arcturus set.

Gull-swift and swerving, the wet spirit freed
Skims the huge breakers. Watching at the prow
Of any southbound vessel, a sailor, heed
Never that petrel spirit, cruel as pride.

Let no cliff-haunting woman, no girl claim
Kinship with Glaucus, neither sow
The tide with daffodils, nor call his name
Into the wind, for he is glorified –
And cold Aegean voices speak his fame.

November 1941

WAR POET

I am the man who looked for peace and found
My own eyes barbed.
I am the man who groped for words and found
An arrow in my hand.
I am the builder whose firm walls surround
A slipping land.
When I go sick or mad
Mock me not or chain me:
When I reach for the wind
Cast me not down:
Though my face is a burnt book
And a wasted town.

March 1942

NOT CHOSEN
(For Milein)

Not chosen but unsure protagonist
Of my father's folly and his father's greed,
I rake the acre that I should have sown
And burn the corn to save next season's seed.

Forgive my heavy hands their new precision
Learnt otherwise than we had wished or hoped;
Look not too closely as I move beside you –
My feet are shackled and my neck is roped.

I am the watcher in the narrow lane –
My tongue is schooled in every word of fear.
O take me back, but as you take remember
My love will bring you nothing but trouble, my dear.

July 1942

AN EARLY DEATH

This is the day his death will be remembered
By all who weep:
This the day his grief will be remembered
By all who grieve.
The winds run down the ice-begotten valleys
Bringing the scent of spring, the healing rain
But the healing hands lie folded like dead birds:
Their stillness is our comfort who have seen him.

But for the mother what can I find of comfort?
She who brought glory out of bone and planted
The delicate tree of nerves whose foliage
Responds freely to the loving wind?
Her grief is walking through a harried country
Whose trees, all fanged with savage thorns, are bearing
Her boy's pale body worried on the thorns.

2nd Lieutenant Keyes, late 1942, a few months before being
sent to the Tunisian Front

Sidney Keyes at War

(Addendum extracted from 'The Rising Flame:
Remembering Sidney Keyes', 2015, Shoestring Press)

KEYES WAS TRANSFERRED IN JANUARY 1943 TO THE 1ST Battalion of the Queens Own (Royal West Kent) Regiment. It was an active service unit. He was assessed by seasoned officers who saw a steadfastness in the awkward young intellectual, and they recommended him to command a platoon of thirty men. Keyes' unit was sent to Tunisia by ship in March to join the Allied effort to crush the remaining German and Italian forces in North Africa. The Notebook and correspondence of the time seem to record a sudden shift in his mood to one of lightness and acceptance. He wrote on ship, "every moment is a state of being *in itself* not a way of transition to the next." He slept well and even slumbered right through an enemy torpedo bomber attack.

"I have never been so little troubled with sex in my life," he wrote, "there are photographs of Milein and Renée over my bed. Is this vanity because they are both so beautiful? But I never dream of them, and rarely think of them for long... the succession of days, like a dream, is infinitely soothing ...".[44] He seems to have enjoyed the unit's brief stay in Algiers and impressed his men by being apparently unperturbed by further enemy air raids and by the tough living conditions. The battalion had arrived on the 22nd March 1943 and were billeted in an old brick factory on the outskirts of the city which he describes in a letter: "everything was incredibly dirty ...the roof leaks and the windows are broken ...the whole area outside is a sea of mud, and we have a noisome swamp a few yards away, where the frogs keep up an incessant roar of croaking night and day."[45] Despite the prospect of imminent action, Keyes maintained his outward serenity and good humour. He took the men of his platoon on an excursion to view the nearby Tipaza Roman ruins and lectured them on ornithology, the Atlas mountains, the natural world and poetry. To them, it seemed that Keyes knew about everything. They enjoyed his talks although much of it "went over their heads".[46] (James Lucas, Memoir, *Sidney Keyes: Collected Poems*, 2002). In a letter to his

---

[44] Notebook entry in Guenther, *op. cit.*

[45] In a letter to Violet Keyes, in Guenther, *op. cit.*

[46] James Lucas, 'Memoir' in *Sidney Keyes: Collected Poems* (2002)

step-mother, Keyes recorded with amusement that, "this afternoon I discovered for the first time that my men call me 'Puss in Boots' partly, I think, because of my appearance and partly because I pad about in rather elaborate crepe-soled fur-lined boots and tend to appear noiselessly at awkward moment (for them) …"[47] There was one discordant note however. He wrote to Renée on March 27th: "I had a strange and most unlucky dream. I dreamt we are being married and saw the actual ceremony. That is said to be one of the most unlucky dreams one can have."[48]

Surely he knew at some level that he wasn't coming back? Herbert Read certainly thought that Keyes was saying goodbye for good when he called to his offices in early 1943 and it is hard not to read inner certainty into poems like "An Early Death" and in "The Wilderness" which has the stanza: "O speak no more of love and death/ And speak no word of sorrow / My anger's eaten up my pride/ And both shall die tomorrow." The O.C.T.U instructors were worried about him and my father just shook his head and said no one was much surprised when they heard what happened later. After all, it was probably well known to those soldiers who listened to his educational talks that infantry platoon leader was one of the most dangerous jobs in the army. "The hardest rank for commissioned officers was platoon commander, because he takes the big patrols out he does everything forward. ….they take the rough edge. There's no doubt about that. A very, very tough job."[49] So commented an infantry N.C.O. of the time Another contemporary soldier noted: "The turnover of platoon commanders was incredible. If you were at all good as a platoon commander and lasted any time at all before very long they would take you and make you a company commander but quite often they were killed or captured or didn't last the course for one reason or another. I wouldn't like to say what the turnover was but it was quite horrific."[50]

---

[47] Letter to Violet Keyes, John Guenther, *op. cit.*

[48] Letter to Renée-Jane Scott in Guenther, *op. cit.*

[49] Peter Hart, *The 16th Durham Light Infantry in Italy 1943–1945* (1991)

[50] Peter Hart, *op. cit.*

I think Keyes still hoped despite the grim outlook. There was certainly no 'death wish'. He wrote to John Heath Stubbs at the time criticizing the thanatic urges of the "necrophilous" Germans: "a whole nation has gone stark mad with the love of death."[51] And to Renée, he described his hopes that he would return to her someday: "The only way back seems to be through armed Europe. I am not in much of a hurry, but I will get back sometime if it is humanly possible; and I have never yet failed to do anything I set myself to do."[52]

The 1st Royal West Kents went up to the front on April 2nd 1943. They travelled by sea from Algiers to Bone in north-eastern Algeria; then they moved by truck to Beja in northern Tunisia. The winter fighting had stabilised near the village of Oued Zarga on the Zarga River where the road led east through Medjez-el -Bab. This area was to be the jump-off point for the Allied spring offensive. The Medjez was the gateway to Tunis eighty kilometres away. It was a strangely green and fertile place for the soldiers that came expecting to see a desert. The valleys were thick with olive groves and wheat fields and wild flower meadows stretched along the slopes that rose up on each side. It was a quiet sector at first, but the dead were not yet buried from the winter fighting and the horizon flickered with gun flashes to the North as 1st Army began to soften up the German bastion on Djebel el Ahmara which later became known as 'Longstop Hill'.

Morale was not particularly high. After the slow progress following the 'Torch' landings' in the previous year and the reverses at Rommel's hands at Kasserine Pass in the February of 1943, 1st Army was seen as inferior and unlucky compared to the glamorous 8th Army 'Desert Rats' beginning to steam-roller the Afrika Korps out of the Mareth Line on the southern front. Still, 1st Army had a dirty job to do and they prepared themselves to get on with it. The coming conflict was later called 'the Battle of the Peaks' as the Allies contested the stubborn remnants of the

---

51 Letter to John Heath Stubbs, Guenther, *op. cit.*
52 Letter to Renée-Jane Scott, Guenther, *ibid.*

Axis Forces across a succession of rocky heights along the valley of the Medjerda valley that led to Massicault and to the open country of the Tunis plains beyond.

At first, Keyes was involved in small scale skirmishing and probing of the enemy lines on the high, bleak Medjerda plateau. This mountain country has been described by General Anderson himself, (commander of 1st Army), as "a vast tract of country, every hill in which is large enough to swallow up a brigade of infantry, where consolidation on the rocky slopes is very difficult, in which tanks can only operate in small numbers, where movement of guns and vehicles is very restricted, and where the Division had to rely on pack mules for its supplies and to carry wireless sets, tools and mortars. The general impression is one of wide spaciousness – a kind of Dartmoor, or Central Sutherlandshire, but with deeper valleys and steeper hills".[53] Keyes' men willingly followed him in those first patrols in that hard landscape – a wasteland like that described in his late poem "The Wilderness" in which the poet speaks of "a last great meeting among mountains / Where the metal bird sings madly from the fire." The "wilderness" of the poem is the external reality of the battlefield that awaits the poet as well as an inner state where the poet steels himself for the coming ordeal – "This is my calling, to seek the red rock wilderness." His men followed him not so much because of his military skill but for his evident steadfastness and his moral and physical courage. James Lucas, who served as a private in Keyes' platoon, wrote of him: "During my Army service, I had a number of platoon commanders. Keyes was the best of them. He was the quiet, determined, non-blustering type of leadership. His manners were impeccable and he did not talk down to us, nor was he condescending... He was a gallant, Christian gentleman..."[54] Despite all the battlefield handicaps of a super-heated intellect and a refined sensibility, Keyes' integrity had shone through to his men and gave them confidence in him.

The Royal West Kents moved forward from Oued Zarga and

[53] Lt. General K. Anderson, 'Official Despatch', *London Gazette*, 1946

[54] James Lucas, 'Memoir', *op. cit.*

occupied the high ground that had been wrenched from the enemy at the beginning of the offensive. The battalion spent their time sheltering in weapon pits they had dug into stony ground on the reverse slopes as the Germans still pounded the ridges with artillery fire. James Lucas recorded that Keyes was "particularly interested in the types of beetles that infested a dead, wolf-like dog that lay unburied near our platoon positions."[55]

Despite the heavy responsibilities of leading his men on active service Keyes remained a keen observer of the natural world. He wrote to Renée: "I am writing this crouched on a hillside somewhere in North Africa not far from the enemy. It is just getting dusk and there are no lights so I shall probably have to stop fairly soon. This is a country of green downland with little hidden valleys where there are farms and water mills, on the bare hillsides, the Arabs drive their primitive oxplows which barely scratch the dirt, and everywhere the ground is covered with a tall purplish flower, like a kind of acanthus, these Arab plowmen wear hooded cloaks made of sacking or some coarse materiel and as they plow behind two white oxen, they look blind and sinister, like figures of death or pestilence...." Keyes must have finished the letter the following morning – "It is now just after dawn, a flock of goldfinches is passing through the willow trees in the valley where I write. I know that, if I come back or get time to think, all these images will return with greater power and never leave me, and all this would have been infinitely worthwhile..."[56]

James Lucas, such a vital witness of these last days (he was later to become a noted military historian and Keeper of Photographs at the Imperial War Museum), described how Keyes seemed to grow in confidence as he crawled through the flowering broom plants in night time patrols between the front lines in the hills overlooking Oued Zarga. Lucas (himself a German speaker) told how on one such reconnaissance patrol, "I suddenly heard my officer speaking German berating someone for sleeping on duty. When Gibson and I closed up Keyes told us that the figure

[55] Lucas, *ibid.*

[56] Letter to Renée-Jane Scott, John Guenther, *op. cit.*

reclining in a very relaxed position on a rock was dead."[57] It seems that Keyes had the presence of mind to pretend that he was a German officer in case that figure had been a live enemy sleeping sentry. Somehow, Keyes had become acquainted with the night and had hardened himself to encountering death there. He seems to have almost enjoyed creeping about under the clear Tunisian starlight in those "crepe-soled boots' that had so startled his men. Lucas also described how his platoon contained some "loud-mouthed types of the 'let me have a go at the Gerry' variety." He says Keyes took the 'loud-mouths' out into German lines under a spectral moonscape and left them there while he crawled away on his own. The chastened men were grateful to see him eventually return and lead them back to safety. It seems that Keyes had discovered in himself a toughness that maybe had always been there. Perhaps he was finally living up to his undergraduate boast he had written to his poet friend, "I am probably less weak than you think and rather more deliberately destructive."[58]

Keyes' battalion held the high ground from 12th April up until the 19th April when they went into a reserve position. Keyes wrote to his step-mother, "Tunisia is like Scotland must have been in the eighteenth century, a mass of bald mountains, terribly cold at night."[59] He wryly described to her how on the night of the 18th he had led a patrol behind German lines in an attempt to locate and destroy a wireless transmitter. He found it, "…exciting. We went out at night, reached the village where the apparatus was supposed to be, without incident, and took cover in a cave… I heard a loud buzzing noise behind me and saw a large wooden box on legs … quite sure I had found the station and would get the MC I went up to it and looked in. It was an enormous beehive! There was …. no wireless station. I shall have to wait a little longer for my MC after all."[60]

This letter shows a boyish bravado, perhaps sheltering his

[57] James Lucas, 'Memoir', *op. cit.*

[58] Letter to John Heath-Stubbs in Guenther, *op. cit.*

[59] Letter to Violet Keyes, in Guenther, *ibid.*

[60] Guenther, *ibid.*

step-mother from the realities of his situation. After all, Keyes' uncle had been killed in 1918 at the age of 24 while winning the Military Cross and Keyes himself had written about the likely fate of the soldier: "It's a long way and a long march to the returning moon and the soil"[61] James Lucas observed that Keyes "had an unusual habit for a frontline infantryman. He lined his slit trench with an American army issue blanket so that no pieces of loose soil fell on him."[62] Perhaps Keyes did not like the touch of the earth. One is reminded of the poet's plea in 'Ulster Soldier' – "let me not be rotted".

Keyes had a brief respite from the front when he was sent behind the lines on an explosives and mine recognition course on the 20th April. During that break from the fighting, he again wrote to a senior officer he knew, asking for a transfer to the Intelligence Corps. He then rejoined the West Kents now back in the new front line east of Medjez el Bab on a notorious stretch of front called 'Banana Ridge'. The Germans had counterattacked across that ground on the 20th April in an offensive with the ironically poetic name – *Fliederblute* – lilac blossom. The German surge had been halted and the slopes around Banana Ridge were still littered with dead men and burnt- out Bren carriers and Churchill tanks. The Germans had consolidated on high ground overlooking an area the British called 'Peter's Corner' (So named, apparently, because you were likely to meet St. Peter if you frequented the spot.[63]

Keyes maintained cheerful letters to Renée, writing to her on the 26th: "I am writing in a tiny shut-in valley among the mountains, with a clear stream in the bottom, and filled with cypresses and fig trees …I can hear the Arabs shouting to their flocks and playing crazily like crickets on their reed pipes. The whole scene is quite perfect, like something staged…I shall have a lot to say about all this when the time for speaking returns. I cannot think that this campaign can last much longer; but after

61 Sidney Keyes, 'The Foreign Gate', written February–March 1942

62 James Lucas, 'Memoir', *op. cit.*

63 David Rolf, *The Bloody Road To Tunis* (2001)

that, who knows?"[64] The letter describes a scene of rustic tranquillity but he adds a sombre after-note telling her that should he be killed he has left instructions that she should have his signet ring. It was to be his last letter to her.

On that same day of writing "A" and "B" companies of Keyes' battalion had attacked the ridge at Sidi Abdallah. They hung onto the high ground in the face of counterattacks but "in the end the position was considered to be untenable ...the cost had been heavy. They included Major Dann and Lieutenant Ashton killed and Lieutenant Besley wounded."[65] The remainder of the battalion, including Keyes, were ordered to make a further attack in the following days.

On the late afternoon of April 28th, 200 men of "C" and "D" companies of 1st Battalion, Royal West Kents descended from Banana Ridge and advanced across the valley overlooked by Point 133, a high feature that dominated the British axis of advance (so named because its crest was marked as 133 meters above sea level on Army maps). Their job was to take and hold that high place. The Germans that faced them were *fallschirmsjager* from 5th Parachute Regiment, hard-bitten veterans from the Eastern Front and the winter fighting in the mountains. They were not going to be giving in easily despite the fact that their army in Africa was facing an overwhelming attack on two fronts.

James Lucas, then just a year younger than Keyes, walked beside his lieutenant as "C" company advanced with "D" company supporting them on the left. Lucas had been given the job of being Keyes' 'runner' – a man who carries messages should the notoriously unreliable radio sets fail. Lucas (who died in 2009) wrote a memoir of Keyes for the 1988 Carcanet edition of Keyes' Collected Poems but what is not so well known is that he had earlier written a fuller and more brutal account of the battle for Point 133 in an obscure military magazine.[66] This account describes the attack in detail and makes much clearer what actually

[64] Letter to Renée-Jane Scott, John Guenther, *op. cit.*

[65] H. Chaplin, *The Queen's Own Royal West Kent Regiment 1920–1950* (1959)

[66] James Lucas. 'Point 133:Tunisia', *War Monthly* (1980)

happened during Keyes' first and last real battle.

Keyes' 14 platoon, "C" company moved along grassy tracks with the rest of the attacking force in the late afternoon of the 28th April. The position they were assaulting had been fortified by the Germans. It was about 2000 yards from the start line in the Medjerda valley below Banana Ridge. All the slopes were thickly sown with wheat – bright green in the intense light and moisture of the Tunisian spring. Point 133 loomed in front of them. It overlooked Sidi Abdallah hill and Cactus Farm, a strongpoint the Germans had protected with concrete emplacements and minefields. The incline steepened and Lucas saw Keyes standing in a knot of officers from the regiment consulting and looking up at the enemy lines as an allied artillery bombardment started up. The shells whistled over their heads to land on the enemy positions on Point 133. "In the early evening light to my magnified sense of vision the flashes from the exploding shells coruscated like giant opals and the sable smoke from the detonations hung in an ever spreading pall over the enemy lines."[67] They waited for the bombardment to end while green and red signal lights rose from the German lines above them. Lucas recorded that he: "realised quite suddenly that I was seeing some, perhaps many of my comrades for the last time."[68].He wrote that he was not afraid of dying as such but was afraid of "being wounded and left in this empty, hilly wilderness."[69]

The bombardment moved further up the slope, Keyes blew a whistle and the men advanced "swishing through long, green grass wet with evening dew."[70] They passed through the slit trenches of the British forward line. Weary men of 2nd Royal Fusiliers, who had been savaged by German counter-attacks in previous days, wished the West Kents good luck as they passed. Colonel Haycraft, the battalion commanding officer, "a tall elegant figure" wearing the regimental forage cap, accompanied them up to the start line,

67 James Lucas, "Point 133: Tunisia", *op. cit.*

68 *Ibid.*

69 *Ibid.*

70 *Ibid.*

calling out encouragement and warning them to keep an orderly advance. "Good going, Percy," he kept shouting to Major Percy Braithwaite who was in command of the attacking force.[71] Lucas recorded that there were no heroic speeches made. He continued next to Keyes who was carrying a Thompson sub machine gun. The barrage moved on, thumping down beyond the crest of the ridge. Their objective was covered in rolling smoke. Lucas heard Keyes speaking to him in "a casual tone" barely audible under the sound of the barrage: "'See that little yellow flag? Well, that indicates that we are in a German minefield… I shouldn't think they have anti-personnel mines here probably only anti-tank… but if you feel an explosion underfoot press down with your boot. There'll be a second explosion and this will take off your leg but that's better than having the mine jump up to waist height and kill us all with ball bearings, isn't it?' I didn't reply and he went on to tell me how to identify the thin wire horns of the S mine fuse but since it was now sunset and not very light it was unlikely that I would be able to detect a small group of pins buried in the ground and in an agony of apprehension I walked alongside Sidney Keyes across the mined area."[72] Keyes was simply repeating the cold-blooded, official advice about "S" mines, or 'Bouncing Betties' as the infantrymen called them, advice he had no doubt learned on his recent mine course.

The line of infantry led by Keyes climbed on through the dust thrown up by the bombardment. Lucas describes how he suddenly encountered a German position with a machine gun on a tripod in front of him. He could see no enemy soldiers but as he jumped across the lip of the trench he saw them crouched at the bottom. He called to his section Corporal, a man called Rudling who was close to him. They both stood over the Germans. Lucas does not spare the reader from a truly terrifying account of what happened next. It seems that the enemy soldiers were so overwhelmed with the shock of the bombardment or because of suddenly encountering British infantry that they made no effort to defend

[71] *Ibid.*

[72] *Ibid.*

themselves. They remained at the bottom of the trench, some pressing their hands into their faces. One man was on his knees facing Lucas: "empty-handed, searching for something in his greatcoat, his face was turned upwards towards me and his eyes dark in the pallor of his face held an expression of absolute horror."[73]

Lucas and Corporal Rudling shot them all then discovered more men hiding in a dug out: "from the darkness came the sound of high-pitched squealing. The corporal and I moved to the long side of the trench and fired into the men hidden in the small cave. The squealing stopped abruptly…"[74]

14 Platoon paused mid slope as the barrage ended and Keyes ordered bayonets to be fixed. He then led them in a last rush to take the ridge. There was a flurry of action and several prisoners were hustled away. Sounds of heavy machine gun fire could be heard in the left distance telling them that "D" company had run into stiffer opposition. On Point 133 however the firing had stopped, leaving the sound of "the cicadas … (which)…were as loud as birds and the swishing of our bodies through the thigh-high wheat was like the sound of surf. A slight breeze dispersed the smoke and dust exposing a clear sky."[75] Major Braithwaite and Keyes and the other lieutenant reorganised the company to form a defensive rectangle on the high ground ready for the inevitable counterattack. Men tried to make holes in the stony soil and whispered together, sharing stories about what had happened during the attack. The company command post at the centre of the position showed a green glow from the radio set and the men could hear the cursing of the signaller when he failed to make contact with brigade headquarters. Those sets were particularly unreliable at night when the signal bounced off the ionosphere. They could hear units thirty miles away but no-one closer at hand. The men of Keyes' unit were on their own.

Keyes was sent forward at 2am with a patrol of nine men from

73 *Ibid.*

74 *Ibid.*

75 *Ibid.*

14 Platoon on the night of the 28th. The remainder of his platoon, including Lucas, remained in the defensive box. Keyes' mission was to probe along the rocky ridges to check for enemy activity and to ward off any patrols or counter attack. Did he perhaps volunteer for the job because of his night time prowess? The small group, led by Keyes, crept out some distance then waited for dawn.

At first light on the 29th Keyes saw Germans moving across their front and sent some of his men back to warn his company commander of a possible counter attack. They seem to have got lost in the undulating shadowy terrain. Keyes himself stayed behind along with his orderly, Lance Corporal Harold Smith (a 32 year old married man from Brandon in Suffolk). Then there was silence. Nothing more was heard of them. Their company was all but wiped out by a fierce German counter attack half an hour later.

Lucas gives a vivid account of the savage confusion of that dawn attack: the weight of fire that suddenly landed on them and the grim efficiency of the German paratroopers' enfilading tactics. Major Braithwaite was badly wounded in the stomach and Corporal Rudling who had shot the squealing Germans was killed. Lucas was captured along with the remnants of his company. He recorded the surreal, almost casual, conversations he had with his captors and his attempts to help a dying British sergeant lying in the wet wheat who had "a very gentle voice and calm expression"[76] Lucas was taken behind German lines to a headquarters area not far from the Tunis road. He was interrogated then released back to the survivors of his company. There was no sign of his missing Lieutenant.

The Royal West Kents tried to retake Point 133 on the 29th[77] then were pushed off it again the next day. After eighteen hours of fighting it remained in German hands. The Medjerda front swung back and forth and Keyes' battalion and whole brigade were consumed in fighting around the nearby strongpoint of Cactus Farm. German paratroopers backed up by Tiger tanks beat

[76] *Ibid.*

[77] Chaplin, *op. cit.*

46

the British off. Hundreds died in the savage infantry fighting. No-one had time or opportunity to search for Keyes, and his unit was too badly mauled for close accounting of the missing. The 1st Battalion Royal West Kents lost sixteen officers and three hundred men that April. The Battalion was too weakened by casualties to do more than guard prisoners for the rest of the campaign but the Medjerda front was broken open soon after and further south 8th Army crossed The Mareth Line and pressed forward to Tunis. By May 5th the Germans were in full retreat and within two weeks Tunisia was in Allied hands.

Keyes never returned from his venture beyond the lines. There is a profound mystery as to what happened to him. John Guenther was told in 1967 by surviving veterans from Keyes' unit that the last anyone saw of Keyes and his orderly Smith was the two men huddled in the rocks "astride a line of German dugouts."[78] They were looking intently towards the enemy and were barely to be made out in the half-light. They seem to have ignored their comrades' signals to retreat. The other men in Keyes' patrol were soon captured along with the rest of "C" Company. They reported that they heard firing after they last saw Keyes but the sound seemed to come from a distance from his last position.

Guenther's account stood for years as the last word on the mystery until James Lucas wrote in his 1980 *War Monthly* article that "Keyes was last seen with another man attacking the enemy with Tommy-guns". He further elaborated in his 1988 Memoir attached to *Sidney Keyes: The Collected Poems*, "Keyes and another man – Smith or Williams 09 – were last seen standing shoulder-to-shoulder firing Tommy-guns at the advancing Germans." At some stage Lucas had presumably spoken to a survivor of Keyes' night patrol.

At the time however, Keyes was officially listed as missing, probably captured. Colonel Haycraft wrote to Violet Keyes in June "I feel … there is no doubt that Sidney is a prisoner of war and probably in Italian hands…"[79] There was a wait of nearly six

---

[78] John Guenther, *op. cit.*

months before Haycraft visited his regimental graves at Massicault and noticed Keyes' name on a grave there. It took a long while after that for the army bureaucracy of death to clarify that nearly two months after the action a Graves Registration Unit had initially found four field graves a mile beyond Point 133 on June 21st 1943. Of those graves, one was for Keyes, and one for his orderly, Smith. There was also an unknown soldier's grave (a blank cross) and one grave marked for a Private W.T. Williams. Williams came from another unit altogether: The 2nd Duke of Cornwall's Light Infantry. According to John Guenther, Williams had been posted as missing on patrol at El Azabi on the 29th April. El Azabi is about four miles from Point 133. Who initially buried Keyes' little group of fallen men, whether British or Germans, remains unknown. Then we have the question of how had Williams joined them and why they all got to be so far beyond Point 133.

No papers or signet ring was found on Keyes' body when it was reburied at Massicault military cemetery (also known as Borj el Amri) some 3 miles away. Lance Corporal Smith's wallet was returned to his wife by Graves Registration thirteen months later but none of Keyes' personal possessions were returned. He had left his Notebook at Banana Ridge and that was sent back to his publishers by someone in his regiment. The last poems that James Lucas reports seeing Keyes writing at Oued Zarga most likely blew away in the Tunisian dust and someone must have pocketed his ring and the watch and compass given him by his step-mother. His lines from "The Foreign Gate" were prophetic: "A soldier's death is hard/ There's no prescribed or easy word/ For dissolution in the Army's books…"

How Keyes' little group had got to be so far into German lines can only be guessed at. The graves were found well outside the operational area of the German Point 133 defenders – 5th Parachute Regiment (also known as the 'Herman Goering Jäger'). John Guenther researched the German military archives in the 1960s and discovered that the first grave site lay "in an isolated area" belonging to a German armoured reconnaissance unit of

[79] *Ibid.*

10th.Panzer Division. James Lucas mentions speaking to German tank soldiers after he was captured and taken back to farmland closer to the Tunis road. It seems likely that the Keyes gravesite was not very far from where Lucas was actually interrogated. Colonel Haycraft later told John Guenther that Keyes must have worked his way deep into German lines before running into trouble. It should be noted that James Lucas in his Memoir to *Sidney Keyes: Collected Poems* mentions that on previous patrols Keyes went "miles" behind German lines.

Somehow, the lost private from the D.C.L.I. also joined them – William Thomas Williams, aged 22 from Porthleven in Cornwall. Guenther speculates in his biography that both patrols had veered miles from their operational areas and met up before being extinguished. I have found a relevant note in the War Diary of 7th Field Company, Royal Engineers, the same unit that cleared the minefield through which Keyes' unit advanced to attack Point 133. The diary clearly states that 2nd Duke of Cornwall's Light Infantry (Williams' unit) were called up to try and retake Point 133 after the Royal West Kents were driven off it on the 29th.[80] So, maybe Guenther was wrong. Private Williams was not at El Azabi but was in fact another victim of Point 133. This possibility is further reinforced by the fact that Williams was listed as being killed on the 30th on his initial grave marker, unlike Keyes and Thomas who were listed as being killed on the 29th. It was as if whoever buried them knew that the D.C.L.I. dead were from the second wave of the British attack on Point 133.

In the night and fog of battle individuals are nothing – they are truly Rilkean *neiman gleich*, resembling no-one. Keyes easily have been obliterated in a dozen different ways: wounded in the first dawn fire fight perhaps and dying in a German back area or taken prisoner then getting hit by shell fire (Lucas, in his magazine article noted that British shells were falling all the time in the German rear positions). Again, they could even have been shot by the Germans after being captured, though that seems unlikely. Lucas says that he was threatened with execution by his German

80 'War Diary', reproduced in T.M Riordan, *The Shiny 7th At War* (1984)

interrogators but that appears to have been a bluff to get him to talk. The courtesies between combatants of the Desert War still prevailed in Tunisia and there were few atrocities. The Germans allowed the wounded Major Braithwaite of the Royal West Kents to be stretchered off Point 133 and the surrender of James Lucas and the survivors of "C" company was readily accepted by the counter-attacking paratroopers. The Imperial War Museum have a remarkable recording of Hans Teske who served as an N.C.O. with 5th Parachute Regiment – the unit that obliterated "C" company 1st Royal West Kents. Teske was based close to Cactus Farm and he received the Iron Cross for rescuing British wounded under fire. His taped memoirs clearly show a comradely regard for his British opponents.[81]

Most likely Keyes' little group were collected up and buried by British prisoners of war under German supervision, probably from the armoured unit mentioned above. Teske describes how this was a well-established practice. He mentions the Royal West Kents and The Duke of Cornwall's Light Infantry as being among many of the "hundreds of dead, hanging on wire or blown-up" on the hills around Cactus Farm[82] I see them as being interred close to where they fell in a fire-fight. Teske describes those night battles as, "darkness – running shadows – stabs of flame then bodies, many bodies on the ground…"[83] I like to think of Keyes rallying a few stragglers, sweeping far ahead of his company positions then falling out of time and beyond all reckoning.

Keyes quoted from the 6th of Rilke's *Duino Elegies* as an epigraph to his own 1942 poem "The Foreign Gate". The Rilke stanza that Keyes picked begins *"Wunderlich nah ist der Held, doch den jugendlich Toten…"*. This Rilke's poem speaks of a young hero who is nearly indistinguishable from the young dead. He is not concerned with survival but keeps on ascending to a special place – "a charged constellation/ his changeless peril's assumed. There few could find him."[84] Keyes lived out those Rilke lines in his

---

[81] Hans Teske, I. W. M. Interview No. 19101. Reel 4.

[82] *Ibid.*

[83] *Ibid.*

journey from Omagh camp to the Tunisian mountains. The knotty Symbolist workings of the poem show Rilke looking on wonderingly as the hero enacts his own dissolution and loses himself in a moment of decision. That's also how I visualise Keyes on Point 133. He reached the end of fear and crossed the "bridge" he writes about in "The Foreign Gate": "See, I have made you a bridge; a trumpet/ You may shame silence with; a slender dovecot / For your returning, pigeoned now with speech/ Instead of Roman ashes…". Michael Meyer quotes from Keyes in his Memoir of the poet in *Sidney Keyes: Collected Poems*: "a restless candle flame rising highest at its moment of extinction." I am not sure where the lines come from, a letter perhaps or notebook, but they seem to me to be the essence of Keyes. I can only hope that when it came the end for him proved "easy, easy as sleep to the lost traveller frozen in the field"[85]

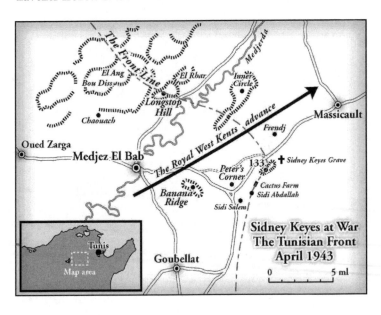

Sidney Keyes at War
The Tunisian Front
April 1943

[84] R.M Rilke, *Duino Elegies*, translated J.B. Leishman & S. Spender (1939)
[85] Sidney Keyes, 'The Snow' (1942)

Bibliography

Anderson, Lt. Gen. Kenneth. "Official despatch by Kenneth Anderson, GOC First Army covering events in NW Africa, 8 November 1942–13 May 1943", *The London Gazette*, 5th November, 1946.

Blaxland, G. *The Plain Cook and the Great Showman.* Purnell, 1977.

Blythe, Ronald. *Talking About John Clare*, Trent Books, 1999

Carson, A. *Eros The Bittersweet: An Essay.* Princeton University Press, 1986

Chaplin, Lieut. Col. H.D. *The Queen's Own Royal West Kent Regiment 1920–1950.* Naval & Military Press, 1959, rpr. 2006.

Guenther, John. *Sidney Keyes: A Biographical Inquiry.* London Magazine Editions, 1967.

Hart, Peter. *Voices From the Front: The 16th Durham Light Infantry in Italy 1943–1945.* Leo Cooper, 1999.

Heath Stubbs, John. *The Divided Ways.* Routledge. 1946.

Higgins, Kevin. *http://pendemic.ie/*, 2020

James, Clive. "Keyes and Douglas". *The Metropolitan Critic.* Faber, 1974. Rpr. Picador, 1995.

Jenner, Simon. "War Poet". *PN Review 149.* Vol. 29 No. 3, January-February 2003.

Kendall. Tim, *The Oxford Handbook of British and Irish War Poetry*, Oxford University Press, 2007

Keery, James, ed. *Apocalypse: an Anthology*, Carcanet, 2020

Keyes, Sidney & Meyer, Michael, (eds.) *Eight Oxford Poets.* Routledge, 1941

Keyes, Sidney. Meyer, Michael, (ed.) *The Collected Poems of Sidney Keyes.* Routledge, 1945

Keyes, Sidney. Meyer, Michael, (ed.) *Sidney Keyes: Collected Poems.* Carcanet, 1988, rpr.2002.

Keyes, Sidney. *The Cruel Solstice.* Routledge, 1943.

Keyes, Sidney. *The Iron Laurel.* Routledge, 1942.

Keyes, Sidney. Meyer, Michael, ed. *The Minos of Crete*. Routledge, 1948.

Larkin, Philip, *North Ship*, Faber 1966

Lucas, James. "Point 133: Tunisia". *War Monthly*, Issue 56, 1980.

Lucas, James. *The British Soldier*. Arms & Armour, 1989.

Lucas, John. *Second World War Poetry in English*. Greenwich Exchange, 2013.

Milligan, Spike. *'Rommel?' 'Gunner Who?'*. Penguin, 1974, rpr. 1976.

Paulin, Tom. 'The Case for Geoffrey Hill' in *The London Review of Books*, April, 1985

Pettigrew, Terence. *Trevor Howard: A Personal Biography*. Peter Owen, 2001.

Piette, Adam. *Imagination at War: British Fiction and Poetry, 1939–1945*. Papermac, 1995.

Rilke, R.M. (J.B. Leishman & S. Spender trans.) *The Duino Elegies*. Hogarth Press, 1939.

Riordan, T.M. *History of the 7th Field Company, R.E., 1939–46*. Self-Pub., 1984.

Rolfe, David. *The Bloody Road To Tunis*. Greenhill, 2001.

Scannell, Vernon. *Not Without Glory: The Poets of The Second World War*. Routledge, 2013.

Tolley, A.T. *The Poetry of the Forties*. Manchester University Press, 1985

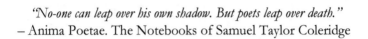

"No-one can leap over his own shadow. But poets leap over death."
– Anima Poetae. The Notebooks of Samuel Taylor Coleridge